First Facts®

SUPER SCARY STUFF

SUPER SCARY STORIES

BY MEGAN COOLEY PETERSON

raintree

a Capstone company — publishers for children

Raintree is an imprint of Capstone Global Library Limited, a company incorporated in England and Wales having its registered office at 264 Banbury Road, Oxford, OX2 7DY – Registered company number: 6695582

www.raintree.co.uk
myorders@raintree.co.uk

Edited by Carrie Braulick Sheely
Designed by Kyle Grenz
Picture research by Svetlana Zhurkin
Production by Katy LaVigne
Printed and bound in China

ISBN 978 1 4747 2067 0
20 19 18 17 16
10 9 8 7 6 5 4 3 2 1

British Library Cataloguing in Publication Data
A full catalogue record for this book is available from the British Library.

Acknowledgements
We would like to thank the following for permission to reproduce photographs: Corbis: Bettmann, 7, 17; Dreamstime: Philcold, 19; Getty Images: Hulton Archive, 9; Newscom: Mirrorpix/Graham Morris, 13, Prisma/Album, 15; Shutterstock: Checubus, cover (bottom), Hurst Photo, cover (bottom left), Lario Tus, 5, 11, Marina Vlasova, cover (top), Nagel Photography, 21, Natalia Lukiyanova/ frenta, 1

CONTENTS

TERRIFYING TALES

You sit around a campfire as your friend tells you about a *ghost* that haunts a nearby house. The hairs on the back of your neck stand up. Your heart pounds. Is the story really true?

People have told scary stories for thousands of years. Some spooky tales are based on real events. Some are completely made up. But they can all give you a good scare!

Why do some people enjoy scary stories? Scientists say they let people experience fear in a safe way.

ghost – spirit of a dead person believed to haunt people or places

THE HOUSE OF HORRORS

In December 1975 George and Kathy Lutz moved into their dream home in Amityville, New York, USA. Fearing for their lives, they fled the house 28 days later.

About a year earlier, Ronald DeFeo Jr had killed his family while they slept. He claimed voices inside the house told him to kill them.

Strange things happened once the Lutz family moved into the home. A *priest* blessing the house heard a voice say, "Get out!" George claimed he saw Kathy floating above the bed.

George said he often woke up at 3.15 a.m. The DeFeo murders were said to have happened around this time. Were the Lutzes being haunted?

Fact or fiction?

Sceptics say George and Kathy Lutz lied about their experiences. Ronald DeFeo's lawyer said he helped the Lutzes make up some of the stories. The book *Amityville Horror* was published in 1977. It was based on the Lutzes' reports. George admitted that some details of the book and a 1979 film weren't completely true.

The book and film about the Amityville haunting became popular. The book sold more than 6 million copies. The blockbuster 1979 film was remade in 2005.

priest – member of a church who leads church services and performs religious rites

sceptic – person who questions things that other people believe in

A GHOSTLY GIRL

The story of the ghostly hitchhiker is a famous *urban legend*. On a cold night, a teenage boy sees a girl standing on the side of the road. She says she just left a school dance and needs a lift home. The boy gives the girl his jacket and drives her home.

The next day the boy returns to the girl's home to get his coat. The girl's mother tells him she died years ago. When the boy visits the cemetery, he finds his jacket. It is laying on the girl's gravestone.

The details of the ghostly hitchhiker story often change. In some stories the driver is a salesman. In others the hitchhiker disappears from the car.

urban legend – story about an unusual event or occurrence that many people believe is true but that is not true

A NOISY GHOST

In 1977 a *poltergeist* was reported in Peggy Hodgson's home in Enfield, Greater London. People said furniture moved on its own. Toys flew through the air.

The scary events soon centred around 11-year-old Janet. While tucked into bed, a force threw her across the room. A man's voice spoke through Janet. It said it was the ghost of a man who died in the house. In late 1978 the ghostly activity quieted, but it didn't stop completely.

The word poltergeist means "noisy spirit" in German.

poltergeist – ghost that causes physical events, such as objects moving

KEEP OUT!

Bluebeard might be the scariest *folktale* ever told. In the story, a rich Frenchman with a blue beard married many times. His wives all disappeared.

The last time he married, Bluebeard gave his new wife a key to a locked room. He told her not to enter it. But she grew curious. When Bluebeard left one day, she crept to the room. When she unlocked the door, she choked back a scream. Bluebeard's former wives lay murdered inside.

One story, many versions

French writer Charles Perrault wrote the most famous version of Bluebeard. But similar tales exist around the world.
In the United States, Bluebeard kidnapped women. He carried them away in a basket. Bluebeard was a king in many versions. In Italy he was an *ogre*.

folktale – story that is told by people over many years
ogre – a cruel giant or monster in stories who eats people

THE EVIL DOLL

In 1970 a woman gave her daughter Donna a ragdoll for her birthday. The doll was called Annabelle. But this was no ordinary doll. People said the toy moved on its own. Blood oozed from the doll. One man said Annabelle left bloody scratches on his chest.

Paranormal researchers Ed and Lorraine Warren examined Annabelle. They said an evil *spirit* controlled the doll.

To this day Annabelle remains at the Warrens' museum in their house. It sits inside a locked case.

ED AND LORRAINE WARREN

paranormal – having to do with an unexplained event that has no scientific explanation

spirit – invisible part of a person that contains thoughts and feelings

TAKEN BY ALIENS?

In 1980 police officer Alan Godfrey drove along a dark road in England. He spotted a *metallic*, oval-shaped *UFO* hovering above the road. Godfrey stopped to call the police station. But his radio wouldn't work.

After a bright flash, Godfrey found himself driving again. But he had no memory of driving away. When he checked the time, about 15 minutes had passed. Had he been kidnapped by *aliens*?

Alan Godfrey was *hypnotized* to help him remember what happened. He said he went inside the UFO. He met a man and robot-like creatures.

metallic – having the appearance of metal
UFO – object in the sky thought to be a spaceship from
    another planet; UFO is short for Unidentified Flying Object
alien – creature not from Earth
hypnotize – to put another person in a sleeplike state

A SPOOKY PRISON

In 1971 Eastern State *Penitentiary* in Pennsylvania, USA, closed. But the spirits of some of its prisoners may have stayed behind. In the 1990s Gary Johnson was working to restore cell block four. He felt someone watching him. But the cell block was empty. Suddenly he saw a black shadow leap across the cell block.

Did Johnson see a ghost? Can evil spirits live in dolls? Have aliens visited Earth? We may never know, but wondering about these spooky tales is part of the fun!

More than 1,200 prisoners died at Eastern State Penitentiary. The prison is considered one of the most haunted places in the United States.

penitentiary – US state or federal prison for people found guilty of serious crimes

GLOSSARY

alien creature not from Earth

folktale story that is told by people over many years

ghost spirit of a dead person believed to haunt people or places

hypnotize to put another person in a sleeplike state

metallic having the appearance of metal

ogre cruel giant or monster in stories who eats people

paranormal having to do with an unexplained event that has no scientific explanation

penitentiary US prison for people found guilty of serious crimes

poltergeist ghost that causes physical events, such as objects moving

priest member of a church who leads church services and performs religious rites

sceptic person who questions things that other people believe in

spirit invisible part of a person that contains thoughts and feelings; some people believe the spirit leaves the body after death

UFO object in the sky thought to be a spaceship from another planet; UFO is short for Unidentified Flying Object

urban legend story about an unusual event or occurrence that many people believe is true but that is not true

READ MORE

Do Haunted Houses Exist? (Do They Exist?), Jenny MacKay (ReferencePoint Press, Inc., 2016)

Ghosts and Other Spectres (The Dark Side), Anita Ganeri (Wayland, 2012)

Ten of the Best Ghost Stories (Ten of the Best: Myths, Legends, and Folk Stories), David West (Crabtree Publishing, 2015)

WEBSITES

The Hampton Court ghosts:
www.hrp.org.uk/hampton-court-palace/history-and-stories/palace-people/ghosts-at-hampton-court-palace

Ghosts at the Tower of London:
www.hrp.org.uk/tower-of-london/history-and-stories/palace-people/ghostsghosts.html

INDEX